CB081793

Lorena Peimbert
Myriam Monterrubio

Bebop 1

Student's Book

MACMILLAN

The Bebop Band

Sing the song: ***The Bebop Band***
Key Language: Eddy, Flo, Leo, Susie, I'm…

Contents

Unit 1 My School

Lesson 1

Listen, point, and say. Sing the song: *Follow Me!* Circle the red crayon.
Key Language: book, chair, crayon, table, red

Lesson 2

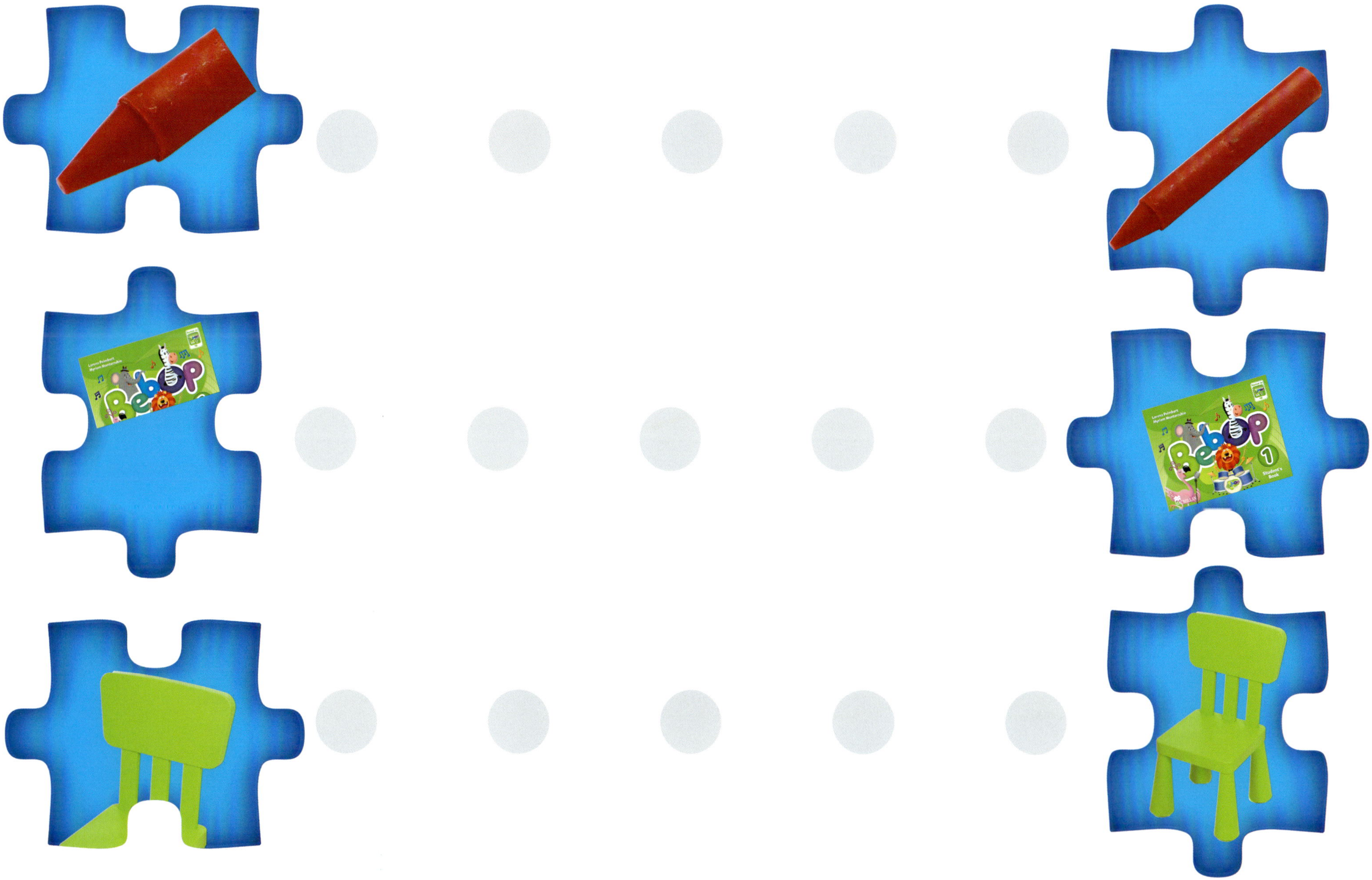

Point and say the school objects. Listen and make fingerprints to connect the school objects. Listen and say with a friend.

Key Language: Look! It's a (*crayon*).

Key Language Review: book, crayon, table

Storysong

Lesson 3

Listen and point to the pictures. Sing the Storysong: *Let's Play!* Count the books in picture 3.
Key Language: 1, 2, 3
Key Language Review: book, chair, crayon, table

Lesson 4

1

2

3

Listen and sing the Storysong. Connect the numbers to the pictures from the story. Trace the circle. p71 **Act out the story with the cut-outs.**

Key Language: circle

Key Language Review: 1–3

Lesson 5

Listen, point, and say. Circle the classroom. Listen and say with a friend.
Key Language: bathroom, classroom, playground, Where's the (*classroom*)? It's there.

Lesson 6

Point and say the places. Look at the pictures and color the correct circle.
Key Language Review: bathroom, classroom, playground

Action Song

Lesson 7

Listen and do the actions. Sing the Action Song: *Musical Chairs*. Count and circle the chairs.
Key Language: stand up, sit down
Key Language Review: chair, 1–3

Lesson 8

Point and say the place. Circle the correct object to complete the picture. p68 **Complete My Progress: Unit 1.**

Key Language Review: bathroom, classroom

Unit 2 My Body

Lesson 1

Listen, point, and say. Sing the song: *Check it Out!* Complete Paul's eyes with blue fingerprints.
Key Language: ears, eyes, mouth, nose, blue

Lesson 2

Point and say the parts of the face. Listen and circle the correct face. Listen and say with a friend.
Key Language: How are you? I'm (*happy*).
Key Language Review: ears, eyes, mouth, nose

Storysong

Lesson 3

1

2

3

4

Listen and point to the pictures. Sing the Storysong: *The Mirror House*. Count the square mirrors in the story.

Key Language: square, 4

Key Language Review: ears, eyes, mouth, nose, circle, 1–3

Lesson 4

Listen and sing the Storysong. Paste blue paper around the correct ending of the story. p73 **Act out the story with the cut-outs.**

Key Language Review: square, blue

Lesson 5

Listen, point, and say. Listen and count. Listen and say with a friend.
Key Language: arms, feet, hands, legs, Look! I have (*two*) (*arms*).
Key Language Review: 2

Lesson 6

Look and complete the face. Point and say the parts of the face. Point and say: *I have* (*two*) (*ears*).
Key Language Review: ears, eyes, mouth, nose I have (*two*) (*ears*).

Action Song

Lesson 7

Listen and do the actions. Sing the Action Song: *Move Your Body*. Point and say the parts of the body.
Key Language: clap, shake, stomp, wiggle
Key Language Review: arms, feet, hands, legs

Lesson 8

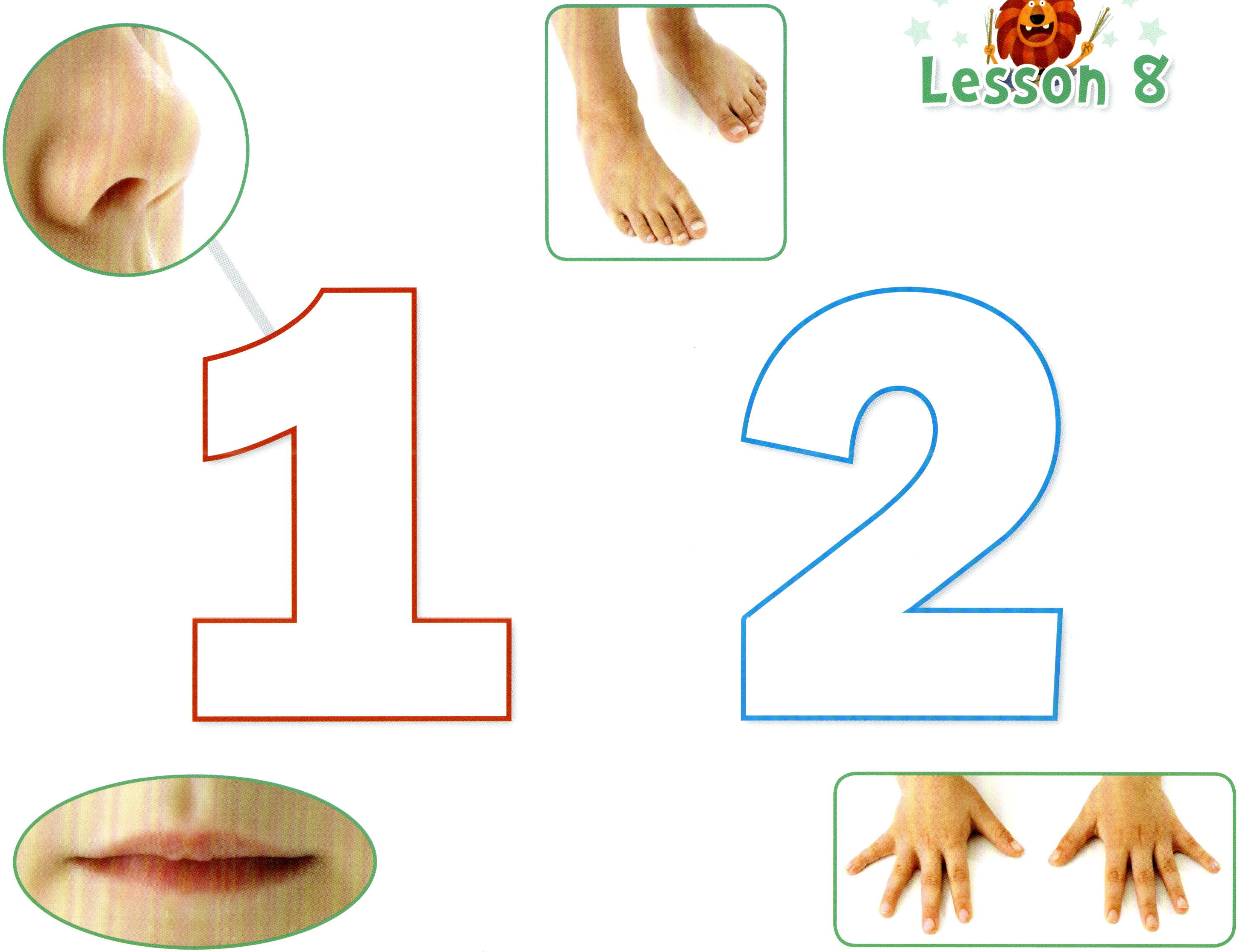

Color the 1 red. Color the 2 blue. Connect the parts of the body to the numbers using the correct color. p68 **Complete My Progress: Unit 2.**

Key Language Review: feet, hands, mouth, nose, blue, red, 1–2

Unit 3

My Clothes

Lesson 1

Listen, point, and say. Sing the song: *What Clothes? What Weather?* Color the sun yellow.
Key Language: raincoat, shorts, sweater, T-shirt, yellow

Lesson 2

Point and say the clothes. Listen and circle the correct clothes. Listen and say with a friend.

Key Language: It's a (*sunny*) day. Put on your (*T-shirt*).

Key Language Review: raincoat, shorts, sweater, T-shirt

Storysong

Listen and point to the pictures. Sing the Storysong: *What a Day!* Count the sweaters in the story.

Key Language: 5

Key Language Review: raincoat, sweater, T-shirt, 1–4

Lesson 4

Listen to the Storysong. Connect the weather to the correct clothes. p75 Act out the story with the cut-outs.
Key Language Review: raincoat, sweater, T-shirt

Lesson 5

Listen, point, and say. Listen and say with a friend. Trace the triangle.

Key Language: boots, pants, shoes, socks, triangle, Where are my (*pants*)? Here they are.

Lesson 6

Count the clothes. Connect the clothes to the shadows. Find and count the triangles.
Key Language Review: pants, shorts, sweater, T-shirt, triangle, yellow, 5

Action Song

Lesson 7

Listen and do the actions. Sing the Action Song: *The Sunny Day*. Point and say the clothes.
Key Language: put on, take off
Key Language Review: boots, shoes, sweater, T-shirt

Lesson 8

Point and name the clothes. Color by number. p68 **Complete My Progress: Unit 3.**
Key Language Review: boots, pants, raincoat, shoes, sweater, blue, red, yellow, 1–3

Unit 4

My Toys

Lesson 1

Listen, point, and say. Sing the song: *My Fun Toys*. Circle the orange ball.
Key Language: ball, car, doll, puppet, orange

Lesson 2

Point and say the toys. Listen and connect the person to the toy. Listen and say with a friend.

Key Language: What is it? It's my (*car*).

Key Language Review: ball, car, doll

Storysong

Lesson 3

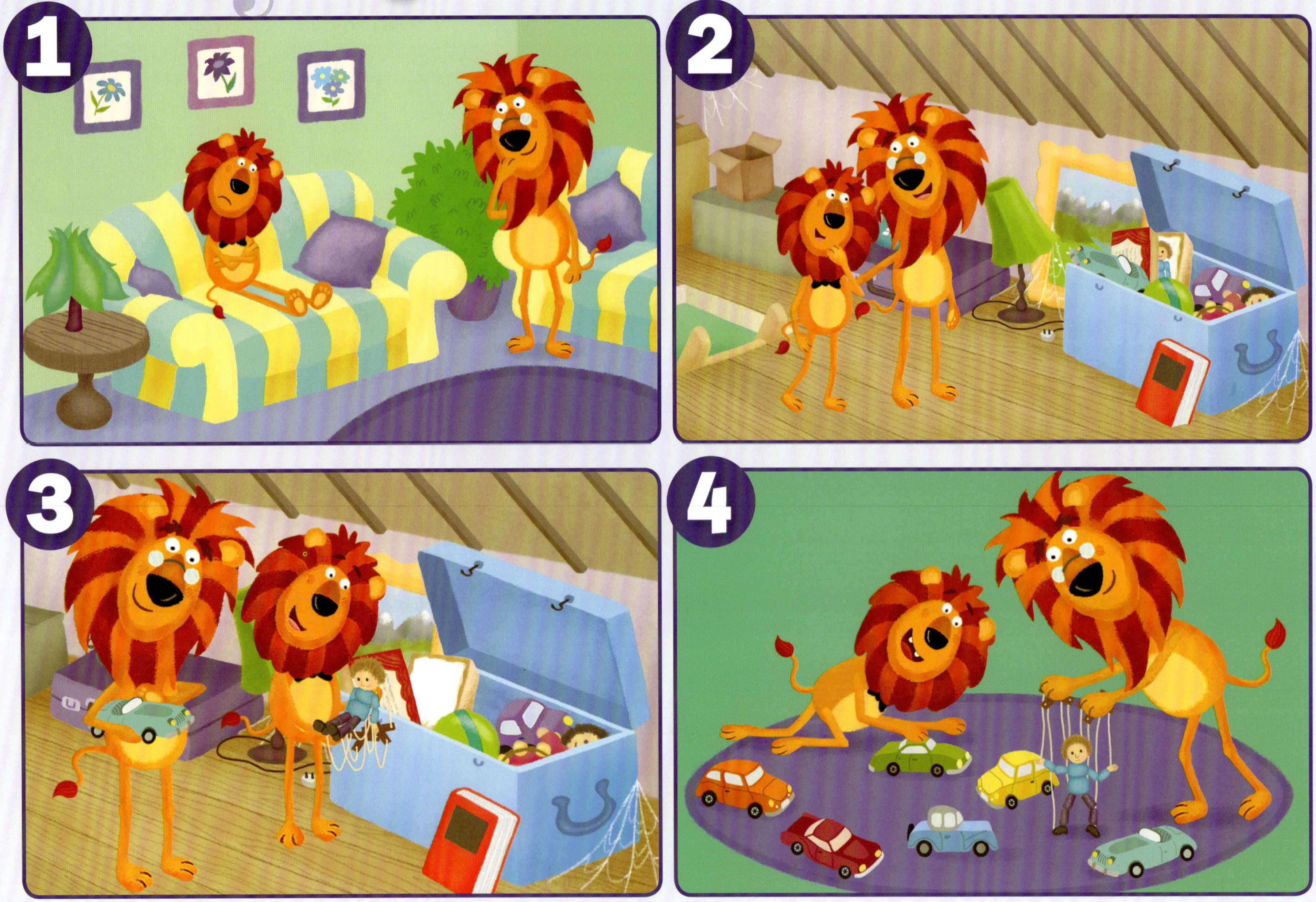

Listen and point to the pictures. Sing the Storysong: *A Day at Grandpa's House*. Count the cars in picture 4.

Key Language: 6

Key Language Review: ball, car, doll, puppet, 1–5

Lesson 4

Listen and sing the Storysong. Circle and say the toys that Leo and Grandpa play with. p77 Act out the story with the cut-outs.

Key Language Review: car, puppet

Lesson 5

Listen, point, and say. Find and say the shapes: *circle, triangle*. Trace the rectangle. Listen and say with a friend.
Key Language: game, teddy bear, train, rectangle, Look! A (*train*). Let's play.
Key Language Review: circle, triangle

Lesson 6

Circle the toys that are old with orange. Circle the toys that are new with blue.
Key Language: old, new
Key Language Review: ball, doll, game, puppet, teddy bear, train

Action Song

Lesson 7

Listen and do the actions. Sing the Action Song: *Playing with Toys!* Find and count the rectangles in the train.
Key Language: playing, riding
Key Language Review: ball, car, doll, train, rectangle, 1–6

Lesson 8

Point and say the toys in the boxes. Find and circle the same toys in the picture. Trace the rectangle. p68 **Complete My Progress: Unit 4.**

Key Language Review: car, game, puppet, teddy bear, rectangle

Unit 5 My Family

Lesson 1

Listen, point, and say. Sing the song: *My Happy Family*. Circle *daddy* and *brother*. Color the plant green.
Key Language: brother, daddy, mommy, sister, green

Lesson 2

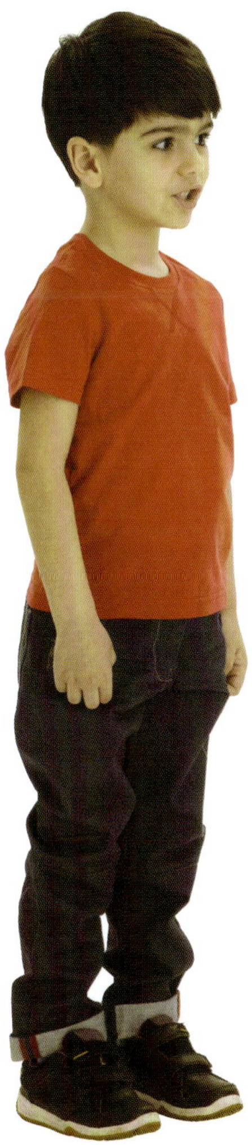

Listen and point to the family members. Listen and circle *sister* with orange. Listen and say with a friend.
Key Language: Who's (*he*)? He's my (*daddy*).
Key Language Review: brother, daddy, mommy, sister

Storysong

Lesson 3

Listen and point to the pictures. Sing the Storysong: *A Family Photo*. Count the animals in picture 4.

Key Language: 7

Key Language Review: brother, daddy, mommy, sister, 1–6

Lesson 4

Listen and sing the Storysong. Complete the family members that are missing. p79 Act out the story with the cut-outs.

Key Language Review: brother, daddy, mommy, sister, ears, eyes, mouth, nose

Lesson 5

Listen, point, and say. Trace the rectangle with green. Listen and circle *mommy*. Listen and say with a friend.

Key Language: bedroom, kitchen, living room, Where's my (*sister*)? (*She's*) in the (*bedroom*).

Key Language Review: bathroom, rectangle, green

Lesson 6

Point and say the family members. Paste green paper on the tree.
Key Language Review: brother, daddy, mommy, sister, green

Action Song

Lesson 7

Listen and do the actions. Sing the Action Song: *At Home*. Count the toys in the picture.
Key Language: cook, play, sleep, wash
Key Language Review: bathroom, bedroom, kitchen, living room, 1–7

Lesson 8

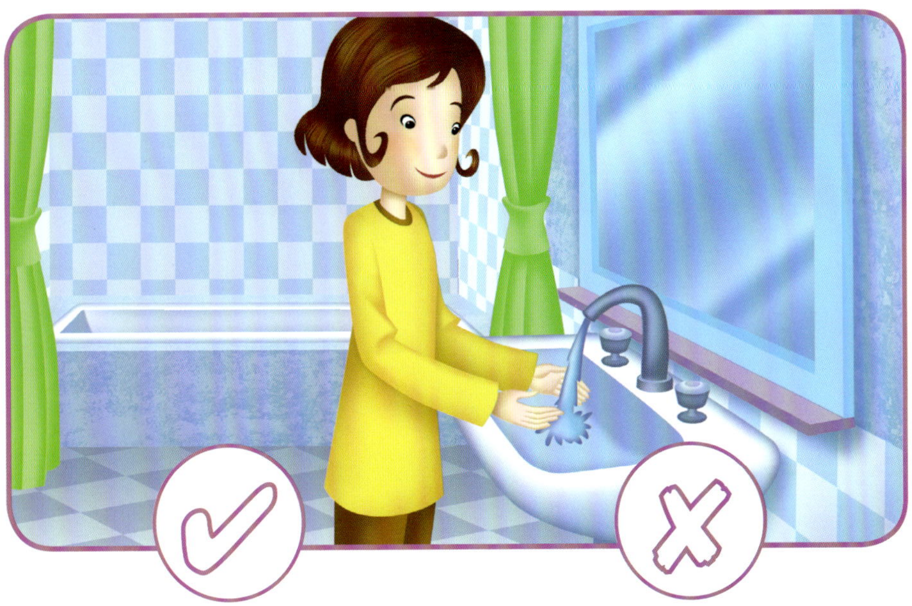

Point and say the family members. Point and say the rooms in the house. Listen and color the correct circle. p69 **Complete My Progress: Unit 5.**

Key Language Review: brother, daddy, mommy, sister, bathroom, bedroom, kitchen, living room, Where's my (*sister*)? (*She's*) in the (*bedroom*).

Unit 6 My Pets

Lesson 1

Listen, point, and say. Sing the song: *I Love my Pets.* Circle your favorite pet with brown.
Key Language: cat, dog, mouse, brown

Lesson 2

Point and say the pets. Listen and color the correct circle. Listen and say with a friend.
Key Language: What pet do you have? I have a (*cat*).
Key Language Review: cat, dog, mouse

Storysong

Lesson 3

Listen and point to the pictures. Sing the Storysong: *Where's my Mouse?* Find and count the circles in the story.

Key Language: 8

Key Language Review: cat, dog, mouse, bathroom, bedroom, kitchen, living room, circle, 1–7

Lesson 4

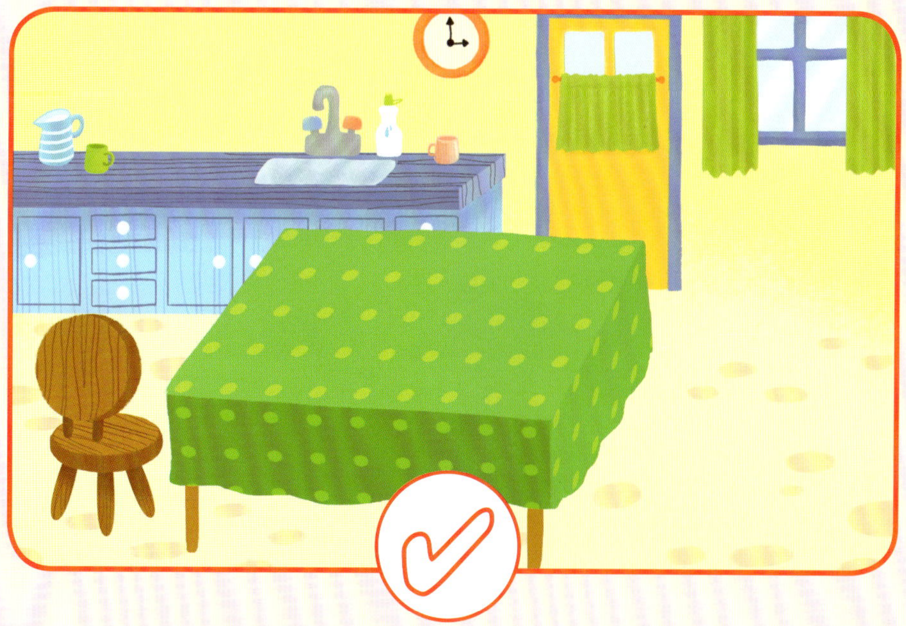

Listen and sing the Storysong. Color the correct circle where Milo Mouse was found. p81 **Act out the story with the cut-outs.**

Key Language Review: mouse, bathroom, bedroom, kitchen, living room

Lesson 5

Listen, point, and say. Circle the brown animals. Listen and count the different animals. Listen and say with a friend.
Key Language: birds, fish, snakes, turtles, Look, (*fish*)! How many (*fish*) are there? (*Eight*).
Key Language Review: brown, 1–8

Lesson 6

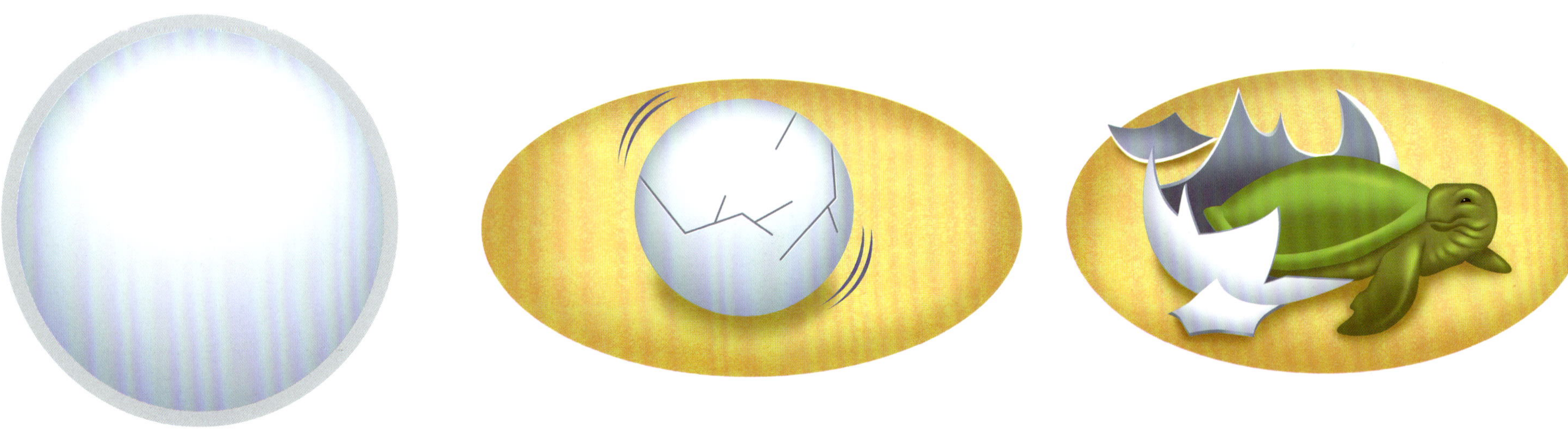

Point and say the animals. Complete the eggs. Paste egg shell on the eggs.
Key Language: eggs
Key Language Review: bird, snake, turtle

Action Song

Listen and do the actions. Sing the Action Song: *Pet Charades!* Circle the animal that Leo is acting out.

Key Language: bend, fly, jump, move

Key Language Review: bird, cat, fish, arms, eyes, hands

Lesson 8

Point and say the animals. Point and say the colors. Circle the animal that's a different color. p69 **Complete My Progress: Unit 6.**
Key Language Review: bird, cat, dog, fish, mouse, snake, turtle, blue, brown, orange, green, yellow

Unit 7 My Food

Lesson 1

Listen, point, and say. Sing the song: *Rub Your Tummy!* Color the grapes purple.
Key Language: apples, bananas, grapes, oranges, pears, purple

Lesson 2

Point and say the food. Listen and connect the person to the food. Listen and say with a friend.

Key Language: What fruit do you like? I like (*bananas*).

Key Language Review: apples, bananas, pears

Storysong

Listen and point to the pictures. Sing the Storysong: *It's Good to Share*. Count the ants in picture 4.
Key Language: 9
Key Language Review: apples, bananas, grapes, oranges, pears

Lesson 4

Listen and sing the Storysong. Look and circle the correct pictures: Who? Where? What? (p83) **Act out the story with the cut-outs.**

Key Language Review: apples, bananas, grapes, oranges, pears

Lesson 5

Listen, point, and say. Listen and trace the shapes for each food. Listen and say with a friend.
Key Language: beets, carrots, peas, tomatoes, (*Tomatoes*), please. Here you are. Thank you.
Key Language Review: circle, rectangle, square, triangle

Lesson 6

Point and say the food. Point and say the colors. Circle the food that's the same color.
Key Language Review: apples, bananas, beets, carrots, grapes, oranges, pears, peas, tomatoes, green, orange, purple, red, yellow

Action Song

Listen and do the actions. Sing the Action Song: *Bananas with Cream and Sugar!* Circle the bananas.
Key Language: add, eat, mix, slice
Key Language Review: bananas

Lesson 8

Point and say the food and colors. Connect the food to the container. p69 **Complete My Progress: Unit 7.**
Key Language Review: apples, bananas, beets, carrots, grapes, oranges, pears, peas, tomatoes

Unit 8 My Town

Lesson 1

Listen, point, and say. Sing the song: *My Town*. Point and say the colors. Circle your favorite community helper.

Key Language: doctor, firefighter, police officer, teacher

Key Language Review: red, orange, yellow, green, blue, purple

Lesson 2

Listen and point. Listen and circle the doctor with purple. Listen and say with a friend.
Key Language: Who are you? I'm a (*firefighter*).
Key Language Review: doctor, firefighter, police officer, teacher

Storysong

Lesson 3

Listen and point to the pictures. Sing the Storysong: *Call 911!* Count the apples in picture 4.

Key Language: 10

Key Language Review: cat, doctor, firefighter, police officer, 1–9

Lesson 4

Listen and sing the Storysong. Look and circle the events that happened in the story. p85 **Act out the story with the cut-outs.**

Key Language Review: bird, cat, doctor, firefighter, police officer

Lesson 5

Listen, point, and say. Listen and circle the school. Listen and say with a friend.
Key Language: fire station, hospital, police station, school, Where's the (*police station*)? There!

Lesson 6

Connect the traffic lights to the police officers. Point and say: *stop* and *go*. Trace the rectangles. Act it out.
Key Language: go, stop
Key Language Review: police officer, circle, rectangle, green, red

Action Song

Lesson 7

Listen and do the actions. Sing the Action Song: *Stand and Shout*. Point and say the community helpers.
Key Language: close, open, shout, stand
Key Language Review: doctor, firefighter, police officer, teacher, fire station, police station, school, eyes, hands, circle

Lesson 8

Point and say the community helpers and the places. Connect the people to the places. p69 **Complete My Progress: Unit 8.**

Key Language Review: doctor, firefighter, police officer, teacher, fire station, hospital, police station, school

My Progress

Color the number after you complete the unit.

Key Language Review: 1–8

5
8
STOP
6
7

Storysong Cut-Outs

Unit 1

Unit 1

Unit 1

Unit 1

Storysong Cut-Outs

Unit 2

Unit 2

Unit 2

Unit 2

Unit 2

Unit 2

Storysong Cut-Outs

Unit 3

Unit 3

Unit 3

Unit 3

Unit 3

Unit 3

Unit 3

Storysong Cut-Outs

Unit 4

Unit 4

Unit 4

Unit 4

Unit 4

Storysong Cut-Outs

Unit 5

Unit 5

Unit 5

Unit 5

Unit 5

Storysong Cut-Outs

Unit 6

Unit 6

Unit 6

Unit6

Unit 6

Unit 6

Storysong Cut-Outs

Unit 7

Unit 7

Unit 7

Unit 7

Unit 7

Storysong Cut-Outs

Unit 8

Unit 8

Unit 8

Unit 8

Unit 8

Unit 8

Goodbye!

Download the Bebop Band app.
See the Parent's Guide in the front of the Student's Book for more information.

Macmillan Education
4 Crinan Street
London N1 9XW
A division of Springer Nature Limited

Companies and representatives throughout the world

ISBN 978-0-230-45292-3

Written by Myriam Monterrubio and Lorena Peimbert

First published 2014

Original design by Macmillan Publishers Limited
Page make-up by Debbie Oatley
Illustrated by Michelle Todd (The Bright Agency) pp2, 4 (insert), 6, 7, 10, 12 (insert), 14, 15, 18, 20 (insert), 21, 22, 23, 26, 28 (insert), 30, 31, 34, 36 (insert), 38, 39, 42, 44 (insert), 46, 47, 50, 52 (insert), 55 (top centre), 60 (insert), 62, 63, 66, 68–87; Ben Mantle (The Bright Agency) pp54, 55, 58; Daniel Griffo (MB Artists) pp4, 8, 9, 11, 12, 16, 17, 20, 21, 24, 25, 27, 28, 32, 35, 36, 40, 41, 43, 44, 48, 49, 52, 55, 56, 59, 60, 64, 65, 67.
Cover design by AM Design Ltd
Cover illustrations by Michelle Todd (The Bright Agency) and Daniel Griffo (MB Artists)
Picture research by Alison Prior

Authors' acknowledgements
Myriam:
To my beloved husband and my two wonderful kids: Majo and Juanpa.
To Lorena: Thank you for your excellent sense of humor. It was refreshing to work with you.
To all the "Beboppers" for making this new dream come true!

Lorena:
To the whole *Bebop* team, for all your hard work in making this project come true.
To my family: Paco, Paquito, Juan Pablo and Ana Lucía. I love you. Thank you for all your support! You're the motor of my life!
To Myriam: Thank you for all the laughter, for all that we have shared, for becoming friends. We're a great team!

The authors and publishers would like to thank the following for permission to reproduce their photographs:
Alamy/David Cook p51(tl), Alamy/Judith Dzierzawa p45(br), Alamy/Erik Lam p51(tc), Alamy/Life on White p51(bc), Alamy/MBI p37(c), Alamy/Ben Molyneux p41(bl), Alamy/Leigh Prather p5(jigsaw piece), Alamy/Tetra Images p61(bl); **Corbis**/Image Source p61(br), Corbis/Radius Images p61(tl); **Getty**/Steve Gorton p51(tr); **Thinkstock**/Dorling Kindersley p11(tr, bc), Thinkstock/Hemera pp5(bl, br), p11(tl, br), p41(tl), 57(peas) 61(tr), Thinkstock/iStockphoto pp41(tr, br), 45(tc, tr, bc), 51(cl, c, cr, bl, br).

Commissioned photographs by **Paul Bricknell** pp5(tl, tr, cl, cr), 11(tc, bl), 13, 19, 21, 29, 33, 37(l, r), 45(tl, bl), 53, 57 (except peas).
We'd like to thank the following for their help with the photos in the book: Annalie, Lucas, Sidrit and Tamzin.

Printed and bound in China

2022 2021 2020 2019 2018
18 17 16 15 14 13 12